The Millionaire Guide

How to Get Rich and *Stay* Rich

DeWayne Wayne

ISBN: 978-1-7377871-0-5

This book was printed in the United States of America.

Table of Contents

Preface

I was inspired to write this book after a routine trip to a local gas station, early one Sunday morning. I stopped in to grab a bottled water, a banana, and gas before my usual morning workout. On my way back to my car, I noticed a guy working for Pepsi pull up in a big blue box truck with a Pepsi logo on both sides. I didn't really pay it too much attention until I got to my car and noticed who had just jumped out of the driver's seat. It was an old acquaintance who happened to be a former NFL player. He and my best friend were cousins, so we had met and hung out a few times before. Despite being raised in the ghetto streets of the South, he had managed to excel in high school football and earn a full scholarship to college. He and I met during his days playing college ball when we were both living in a small college town in Nebraska. Since then, he had become a big deal around town—the local football star.

He went on to sign a multi-million-dollar contract to play football in the NFL, and I didn't see him again for the next decade. But here he was, pulling up in the Pepsi truck and jumping out of the driver's seat. I couldn't believe it.

If only he had been given the right information, I thought.

He had figured out how to earn millions of dollars playing football in the NFL, but was never taught what to do with the money after he earned it.

I skipped my workout session that morning and went back home inspired. I told my girlfriend that I was going to write a book to give people the right information for how to create financial freedom.

Following the process outlined in this book may seem easy. That's because it *is*. Using these methods, I have created financial freedom in my own life. That's why I'm certain they will work for you.

Introduction

In *The Millionaire Guide: How to Get Rich and Stay Rich*, my goal is to walk you through my journey of creating financial freedom, hoping to show you how anyone can do it—regardless of who you are, where you're from, or what you do to earn your money. There is only one way to create financial freedom, the problem is, most people are never taught how.

I have made it my life's mission to help as many people as I can. I have come across so many individuals who want more and know they can do more and have more. Most people I know who have figured out how to earn money—specifically a lot of money—were never taught what to do with money after they earned it. Others think they can never create financial freedom if they work a 9:00 to 5:00 job. As a result, they end up working or hustling for money forever. Or they go broke.

This book is intended to give you a plan to attain financial freedom, a reason to make lots of money, and a way to discover your purpose in life. Not having a solid plan will cost you a lot of money and time. My goal was to write this book without a bunch of big words so that just about anyone could understand it. My only hope is that this book helps you, no matter what your current financial condition is. There are only three things I would like you to do: (1) keep this book until you have reached financial freedom; (2) get another copy and give it to a friend; and (3) as soon as you have created financial freedom, help others to do the same. As I say all the time, we can't do what we don't know.

Chapter 1
Go Get Money

Creating financial freedom is quite easy if you ask me. If you were born without a silver spoon in your mouth or some sort of great talent, it's your duty and responsibility to *create* wealth and financial freedom in your life. If not for you, do it for your family. You can't save your way there, and you can't luck up on it. You must intentionally create freedom and wealth in your life.

It starts with *you!* I often ask my peers two very important questions: (1) How bad do you want financial freedom? and (2) what are you willing to do to get it? Your financial freedom will be based solely on the decisions you make with the money you earn. The key is to be smart with money.

Before you can truly begin to focus on creating wealth and financial freedom, you have to *know* that they are possible, and you must be willing to do whatever it takes to obtain them. It is very important that you not only write your goals down for both the long term and the short term, but you must also develop a solid plan to achieve those goals. I will help you with that as we continue through this book.

If you are anything like me, having to *create* wealth and financial freedom from nothing—no money, no resources, and no support—you must start by creating some income. In my opinion, that is the most difficult part of creating wealth. More than 76 percent of all Americans have chosen to exchange their time for money by working at a job. Some others learn how to sell. Most people assume that they cannot create wealth with a job, but having a job is not the problem. The problem is, the job is just one source of income that requires skill and time. That's called *earned income*. But you will also need *passive income* coming in if you want to create wealth and financial freedom.

In the past, I worked quite a few jobs.

However, it didn't take me long to realize that if I ever wanted to create wealth and financial freedom for myself, that would be difficult with just a job alone. The job would require too much of my time and not bring in enough money. Learning how to sell will speed up the process of creating financial freedom. I began to sell a product as a side hustle. The key for me was to get good at my job and make as much money from it as I could, so that I could then take that money and use it to fund my side hustle. My goal at the time was to get the income from my side hustle to exceed the income from my job.

Eventually, I was making four times as much money from my side hustle as I was making from my job. At that point, I began to realize just how valuable my time really was. The key is to use your time wisely. It's your most valuable asset, and you only have so much of it.

After some point, I was able to walk away from my 9:00 to 5:00 job and focus on my hustle full-time.

Chapter 2
Money Is a Tool

Here is the tricky part—the stage of the game where most people start to lose focus. The money from the full-time hustle starts to get good. However, I want you to know that making money is only the steppingstone or the tool to creating wealth and financial freedom. What you choose to do with the money *after* you have earned it is the most important factor in creating wealth and financial freedom.

The secret is to earn money, and then use that money to make you more money. You want to get your hard-earned cash working harder for you than you work for it. This is not the time to start buying houses, cars, expensive clothes, jewelry, or anything else that depreciates in value. Only buy things that pay you. Ask yourself these questions before making a purchase: Will this pay me? Will this help me to make more money? Can I write this purchase off on my taxes? If the answer to any of these questions is no, the item may be something that can wait until you achieve financial freedom. *Stay focused!*

This stage of the game is going to require a lot of self-discipline. If you have a clear plan for where you are headed in your life, this stage of the game will be fairly easy. It's when you don't have a plan or a purpose for your money that you start to lose track of your finances. This book should be your one and only plan!

Unfortunately, most people who come from backgrounds and circumstances that are similar to mine will figure out how to earn a lot of money, only to get caught up in buying materialistic items to impress others. Being foolish with money and buying depreciating assets will make it very difficult for you to ever create financial freedom. *You have to stay focused on the plan!* The temporary gratification that comes from owning material possessions is simply not worth your financial freedom. It doesn't matter if those possessions are designer clothes, expensive watches, luxury cars, high-end jewelry, or whatever. The key is to wait until you have accumulated enough passive income to start indulging in those things.

Chapter 3
Know Where You're Going

It is very important that you know your out route. By that I mean, start planning for your future very early on in your hustle, or as soon as you begin to earn money. You must know where you're going. Keep in mind that freedom is the ultimate goal.

By the time I was 22 years old. I was making a lot of money. However, I had no clue about how to use that money. I began to spend a lot of it on material things that I thought made me feel good. I thought I was living the life. Everything that I purchased was driven off ego and pride. I bought things that made me stand out. I wanted to be *the man*. I began to become popular among my peers. People began to treat me differently because I had money. I felt as if I were in control of my life.

I often wondered how long that lifestyle

would last. I knew I couldn't do what I was doing forever, nor did I want to. I would often tell myself, *Oh, well, I'm young. I'll figure it out eventually*.

By that time, I had graduated from high school and attended a few colleges. School gave me general knowledge about all kinds of subjects, but it did not teach me what to do with money after I earned it or how to use it to create wealth and financial freedom.

The money I was making was quite noticeable by that time. One person who noticed the money I was making was a friend of mine, the guy I was getting my products from to sell. I'll call him "Ant," which is short for Anthony. Ant was ten years older than me and seemed to be a bit more mature and sophisticated than I was at that time. One thing that struck me about Ant was that he was making a lot more money than I was, but appeared to be worth less. In other words, he didn't show off his money the way I did. The clothes he wore weren't super expensive. He didn't drive a fancy car. In fact, everything about the way he spent his money was completely different from how I spent mine. He presented himself as a normal casual guy. But he was actually using most of his money to purchase real estate, something I knew nothing about.

One day, I went to Ant's home to re-up on my product. Typically, I would pull into the alley at the back of the house, he would come out his back gate, reach into my window, we would exchange money and merchandise, and I'd be on my way. But this day was different. Before I went over there, he invited me to come inside his house. When I pulled up to the front of his house and parked in his driveway, that was something I had never done before. I felt privileged and honored that he would even allow me in his home, and was proud that I had conducted myself in a way that made him feel he could trust me. I wasn't sure *why* he invited me in; I just figured he was tired of coming outside to meet me.

When I walked into his house, I was immediately impressed by the décor. It had a modern look and felt like a place you could actually call home—unlike any place I had ever lived. I felt inspired.

I need to live like this, I thought.

Ant offered me something to drink, but I politely declined, since I was still wondering why he had invited me in. I followed him into the living room and sat down on the couch as he sat on a sofa next to me and began to explain why he had invited me over.

"I've been noticing all the money you're making," he said.

At that time, I was earning ten to fifteen thousand dollars a week.

"You should be investing the money you're making," he continued, "and using it to create passive income."

"What's passive income?"

"Money that you don't have to do anything for. Instead of buying things that lose value as soon as you buy them, you should buy assets that protect your money and appreciate in value over time. If you ever want to get rich and *stay* rich, you need to buy income-producing assets that pay you. Then you can use the money from those assets to buy the material things that make you feel good. If you don't learn to invest your money, you will be hustling forever…, or until you get caught!"

His words made me curious about investing. After all, if there were a possibility that I could get rich from it, I was all in.

Chapter 4
Assets Come First

After twelve years in grade school and high school, and four-plus years attending college, I had never learned about or been introduced to investing. School had taught me absolutely nothing about how to get rich and become financially free. Up until this time in my life, at age 22, I had no idea of what an asset was. I had never even heard the word.

After talking with Ant about investing, something that he said stayed with me until this day.

"Rich people," he said, "buy assets first, poor people buy liabilities first."

"What the heck is an asset anyway?" I asked.

"It's very simple," he said. "Assets put money in your pocket, liabilities take money out of your pocket."

That sounded interesting, so I kept listening.

"The key to life," he continued, "is to take your hard-earned money, no matter what you do to get it, and use that money to create passive flows of income. That's the only way to create financial freedom."

After more discussion about investing, Ant offered me an opportunity I couldn't refuse: the opportunity to partner with him and start putting my money to work. I knew from some past conversations that he was in the real estate space, but to what degree I didn't know at that time. He eventually informed me that he and his family owned a 30-unit apartment complex, which was cash-flowing every month. In time, I came to understand how his system worked.

Ant owned a real estate company that would find, buy, and manage apartments in great locations. Then he would allow friends and family members to partner with him as passive investors. Everyone who invested in the apartment deals received the same benefits as the actual owner. So, in a sense, they were all part owners.

In detail, the way it worked was, first off, every investor's money was protected by a hard asset, a building, that everyone could see and feel. Second, each investor received a 6 to 8 percent preferred return annually, which was distributed every month. Third, each partner's investment had the potential to appreciate over time because apartment buildings always either continue to increase in value or at least hold their value, even in recessions. Finally, there was a 65/35 split on all profits associated with the properties. That meant that Ant's company got 35 percent of the profits, and the investors divided up the other 65 percent.

For example, if Ant's company bought an apartment building for $5 million with ten investors and sold the building ten years later for $10 million, 35 percent ($1.75 million) of that profit went to Ant's company, and the remaining 65 percent ($3.25 million) was divided by the ten investors.

My money would be protected, meaning that

I could never lose it. I would receive a return on my investment every month, and there was the possibility for a big payday in the future once the property was sold or refinanced. And that doesn't include other benefits that I learned about later, such as leverage and tax benefits.

By the time Ant was done explaining the process of investing to me, I had lots of questions. To begin with, I wanted to know how much money I needed to start investing with him.

"Five thousand dollars minimum," he said.

"How long will it take for me to achieve financial freedom?"

"That depends on how much and how often you invest. But with the money you're making, it shouldn't take long."

"Can I get rich and stay rich forever?"

"Without a doubt. This is no get-rich-quick scheme. This is long-term investing in actual real estate. Don't do the get-rich-quick, do the get-rich-for-sure!"

At that point in my life, I didn't have the know-how, the credit, or the time to buy my own real estate, since I was too busy chasing money. Thus, I was eager to partner with Ant and start investing with him.

However, I still had a few unanswered questions. For example, "How long will it take for me to see a return on my investment?"

"As soon as I close on the property. In this case, since I already own the property, you will get a check in a month."

"How often am I allowed to invest?"

"As often as you want."

That was all I needed to know. I was eager to start immediately.

When I left Ant's house that day, I had a plan and a purpose. I drove straight home to get $5,000 and drove straight back to drop off my very first investment with Ant. I started small because I was still a bit skeptical. Nonetheless, I would now be part-owner of a thirty-unit apartment complex that paid me every month while I waited for the appreciation in the future.

Chapter 5
Hustle to Invest

I knew that $5,000 would not create financial freedom for me. I would need to invest a lot more money for that. Up to this point in my life, I had been living recklessly, spending money as fast as I made it. I partied every weekend, took trips all over the country, and spent tons of money trying to keep up with the Joneses. But everything I bought was no good for me. My spending habits were terrible.

A month after I gave Ant my first $5,000 investment, I received a check in the mail from Ant's real estate company for twenty-five whole dollars! At that time, I was making $1,500 to $2,000 a day from hustling, but for some reason, that little twenty-five-dollar check made me feel great.

To the average person, $25 may not seem like

a lot of money, but to me it was a start. The reason it felt so good was that I didn't have to do anything to earn it. It came automatically, requiring no time, knowledge, credit, or effort from me. I took that check straight to the bank, opened my first bank account, and told myself I would never touch that money. I wanted to grow it.

Then I phoned Ant and told him how excited I was about the payment. He reassured me that he still had my initial investment, and it would never go away.

"That payment," he said, "is just the first of many to come. You can expect to receive a check in the mail every month forever, or until we sell the property."

That's all I needed to hear.

By that time, the year was 2006, and I had managed to save up $20,000, part of which I spent on a car I had been wanting—a 1980 Chevy Caprice Classic that I bought straight off the showroom floor. It had 40,000 original miles on it, and I was in love with that car! I bought it for

$5,000 and drove it straight to a tire shop to put some big rims on it. At that time, having big rims on your car solidified your street creditability, so I bought some twenty-six-inch rims, which were the biggest in town at that time, which cost me an additional $10,000.

From the tire shop, I drove directly to a car audio store, where I bought the loudest speakers in the place. This cost me another $5,000. All of that was ridiculous, but you couldn't tell me that at the time. I felt like I was the man, on top of my game.

Without any real knowledge of money, I thought I had everything figured out. But a month later, when I received my second check from Ant for another $25, it didn't take me long to realize I needed to get that number up. After taking that check to the bank, I called Ant up and told him I wanted to invest another $5,000.

"You're a smart guy," he said.

That was my second investment as part-owner of a 30-unit apartment complex. Making those investments made me feel as if that was the only thing I was doing right in my life. It felt good to invest money. The feeling that I got from spending money on investments was completely different from the feeling I got from spending money on materialistic items. The money I spent on investments was paying me every month. On the other hand, every time I bought materialistic items, my money disappeared. Every time I bought investments, my money was protected and paying me. I was on to something.

Chapter 6
Make "For Sure" Bets

After a few more $5,000 investments, I began to start making it a habit to invest $5,000 with Ant every week. If I wanted to ever be financially free, I needed to increase my passive income. While I was still making $10,000 to $15,000 a week from hustling, that money required my time and energy. If I didn't get up to hustle every day, I didn't make a penny. Hustling also required me to risk my freedom every single day. So that was a dead end. If I hadn't started investing, I'm sure I would either still be hustling or in jail. Or even worse, dead. I knew I couldn't hustle forever, so investing was my exit strategy. I began to hustle only to invest. By now, I was less interested in using my money to show off and more interested in protecting my future.

Every time I drove past the apartment

complex that I had invested money in, I always reminded myself, *As long as that apartment building is there, with people paying rent, my money is safe and protected.*

The cash flow from that asset could not be easily interrupted, which made that investment completely different from any other available to me. This was a for sure bet—the easiest way for me to create financial freedom for myself. If I kept investing, I would be financially free in no time. And freedom was my goal.

At that time, the stock market was up and down every day, and I knew that I *never* wanted to lose money. I had become a coward when it came to money. I didn't want to gamble with my money or play games with it. I had a purpose and a goal. The stock market was more drama than I needed. It just wasn't a for sure bet. The chances of me losing money in the stock market were substantially greater than losing money from a real estate investment. It just made no sense to me. I knew nothing about stocks, except that I would buy some, and then cross my fingers, hoping that something great happened. I would have no control over that money. It would be no different than taking money to a casino, hoping to hit the jackpot. And even if I did hit the jackpot, then what? How many times could I do that? And what would I do with the money after I won? I just didn't want to take that kind of risk with my money. If I were going to create financial freedom, I had to do it intentionally. I knew I couldn't get there on luck.

All my life up to that point, I considered myself a risk-taker. However, when it came to my money, I was the biggest coward on Planet Earth. I *never* wanted to lose money. I would rather have risked my life than my money. I had a plan. I was determined to be free. I was committed to living life on my own terms and never have to work or hustle for money again. Freedom was the goal.

Chapter 7
The Holy Grail

After a few years, I was technically broke, since I had forced myself to be illiquid. I didn't want cash. I wanted cash flow. I was converting almost all the money I was making into hard assets that produced income for me. I had come to realize that if cash were king, cash flow is the holy grail. The more money I made, the more money I wanted to get rid of to get working for me. I have always been the type of person who, when I find something I like, I go all in. I become obsessed. I was obsessed with investing and growing my passive income. It's all I was focused on at the time. The materialistic things I used to buy no longer interested me. The desire to spend money to impress other people was gone. I still liked nice things; they just weren't as important to me as they once were. I was now playing the real game of life. I was winning.

By this time, I had grown my passive income from Ant to $2,500 a month, so I still had a ways to go to achieve financial freedom, but I was well on my way. Then, one afternoon, when I checked the mailbox to pick up my usual monthly distribution check, to my surprise there was a check there for $350,000 made out to me. That was indeed the biggest check I had ever seen in my life. But not sure if it was some sort of accident, I immediately called Ant.

He explained to me that he had refinanced the property, and, as a result, he was able to give all the partners their original investments back.

My next question was, "Okay, so what happens now to my monthly payments?"

"We still own the property," he said, "so everyone will still receive monthly distributions. And the best is yet to come when we sell the property."

So, now I had *no* money in the deal, would still be getting paid for the deal, and the best was yet to come.

I was sitting around with $350,000 in cash, and could think of a million things I might want to buy. However, if I touched a penny of that money, I would have to pay a good percentage of it to the government for taxes. That's when I remembered a conversation I had had with Ant.

"Rich people don't pay taxes," he said.

Until then, I never really knew what those words meant. By this point, Ant was not only a friend of mine, but he had also become a mentor. I could call him up anytime to ask about anything. This guy was changing my life in ways that I could never have imagined. He was making me rich, and we were beginning to hang out more often. Everything in my life was going great financially.

As I pondered what I should do with the money, I decided to call up Ant again. As soon as he answered, I said, "Ant, what do I do with this money, and how do I keep from paying a boatload of taxes?"

"You have two options," he said. "You can keep the money and buy whatever you want, but pay taxes on that money, or you can transfer every penny directly into another deal and not have to pay a dime in taxes."

I was still making a lot of money from hustling, and I was also still receiving passive income every month from my investments, so I really didn't need more cash. What I needed was more cash flow. I knew that Ant had another apartment deal he was looking to make—another thirty-unit apartment complex in a very nice location, and the building was already 95 percent occupied. The price for it was around $5 million, of which $2 million would be needed as a down payment. I had a few friends who lived in that particular complex, so I was pretty familiar with the property.

Ant's strategy was to purchase a nice apartment building in a great location, and add value to the property by fixing it up. Then he would raise the rent of each unit and refinance the property to pull out the investors' money. I trusted what he was doing, since it made perfect sense to me. Within a day or two, I reinvested the entire $350,000 with Ant with a smile on my face. My goal was financial freedom.

Chapter 8
No Time, No Credit, No Knowledge

I would often think to myself how great it would be to own my own real estate. Unfortunately, at that time, I didn't have the time, the credit, or the knowledge I needed to purchase my own deals. I was living too fast as it was. There was such a demand for the product I was selling that I never had time to do anything else but make money. I knew very little about credit and how to establish or use it. Although Ant was giving me a little knowledge about the real estate game every now and then, I still didn't have half the knowledge I needed to buy my own properties. After all, I was satisfied with continuing to set up my future and keep increasing my passive income.

Ant had his strategy, and I had mine. My plan was to continue to hustle and keep investing as much as I could in Ant's deals. At that time, my living expenses were $5,000 a month, which adds up to $60,000 a year. My goal was to invest $1 million with Ant, who would then pay me $60,000 a year in passive income. That would be money that I would have to do nothing to earn, and it would come in automatically every month. In other words, the sooner I could get $1 million invested, the sooner I would be financially free. That was my main goal. At that time, in 2010, $60,000 a year was a lot more than most people made at their regular jobs—not to mention that there was almost no way I could lose money, since the properties were always insured. As a matter of fact, my investments were constantly increasing in value.

So, I continued to hustle in order to invest. The income I was making from my first investment was all profit by this point, since I no longer had any money in that deal. My monthly distributions almost paid for all my expenses.

However, I knew that, at any given moment, something could happen to me that could cause me to never be able to hustle again. Whenever that thought ran through my mind, I became even more motivated to keep pouring all the money I was making from my hustle into real estate. My hustle was not for sure. Real estate was.

I was using the income from my monthly distributions to pay for my lifestyle. I took trips, went shopping, and bought whatever I wanted with the passive income I was earning. But I was using all the money I was making from my hustle to invest in real estate.

Most of my friends at that time were caught up in the lifestyles that they were living. I would try to convince them every now and then to start investing like I was, but it always went in one ear and out the other. When I would tell them that all they needed was $5,000 to start, they would always reply, "What do I get for my five thousand dollars?"

I would always try to explain that they would start out making $25 a month, and that's where I lost them every time. It just never made sense to them. I would always try to get them to understand that it's a long game, not a get-rich-quick scheme. I would tell them that it takes time to create financial freedom, but they didn't care to listen. They looked at me as if I were somehow trying to scam them. I guess their logic was, "If I'm spending five thousand, I want something in return that's worth five thousand."

So, for the most part, I kept my investing habits to myself.

Chapter 9
The Financial Freedom Formula

After ten years of hustling and investing, it became apparent to me that I would never have to work a job or hustle for money for the rest of my life. My investments would pay me forever. Furthermore, my investments would also pay my children passive income long after I was dead and gone. In those ten years, I managed to invest over $2 million in real estate and am now financially free. My money now works harder for me than I had to work for it.

Looking back, it was a lot easier than what most people think. First, I had to figure out how to get money. Then I had to find a safe investment vehicle that would protect my money, pay me a consistent and dependable return, and have the potential to appreciate over time. If it hadn't been for Ant, I would never have discovered this method on my own. He taught me how to use money as a tool to create financial freedom.

Through the years, I have come across many people who have earned a lot of money. Some have become great entrepreneurs, creating big businesses that make them millions of dollars. Some have gone on to work for major companies that pay them big bucks. I have known street hustlers who have become self-made millionaires. The one thing that most of these people have in common is not knowing what to do with their money after they earn it. They were never given the knowledge they needed to create financial freedom. Most of them exchange their hard-earned cash for big houses, fancy cars, and nice jewelry. Others spend their lives working and paying bills on the liabilities that have kept them from creating financial freedom. I know they need the information in this book.

Financial freedom has given me the ability to

focus on my true passion, which is helping people. As soon as I realized I was financially free, I began to seek knowledge. I read books, attended seminars, took online courses, walked properties, analyzed deals, and learned the real estate game inside out. I had finally realized my purpose. My past goal was to create financial freedom, and my present purpose is to help other people to do it, too. I want to create the same opportunity for others that has been afforded to me. I want to help people to live a financially free life. Think of how great it would be to never have to worry about money again—perhaps never have to get up and go to work for money or hustle another day. Financial freedom gives you time to do the things that make you happy. You were put here to be happy and to do what makes you happy. However, to achieve that happiness, you must *create* freedom and time.

Most people think that money is the goal and are caught up in trying to make as much money as they can. While making a lot of money is important, the goal should be freedom. The secret that no one ever tells you is, "You must make smart investments with the money you earn if you want to create wealth and financial freedom."

If you have figured out how to earn money, you want to invest it in hard assets that produce a lot of income and have the potential to appreciate over time. That's the only way to achieve financial freedom. I chose multifamily commercial real estate as an investment vehicle to safely store my money and grow my passive income. If you do not invest your money, you will have to work for money or chase it *forever*.

Finally, I would like to leave you with a formula that I discovered, which will determine exactly how much money it will cost you to achieve financial freedom:

First, take your monthly expenses x 12. Then divide that number by your expected rate of return.

The number that results from this formula

will be the amount of money you must invest in order to achieve financial freedom and never have to do anything for money again. Your job will be to find the right vehicle to protect your money, pay you a consistent and dependable return, and have the potential to appreciate over time. That is your goal. That is what you should be working or hustling for. Work hard and hustle for money to be able to exchange that money for freedom. Freedom is the goal.

What nobody ever tells you is that your freedom is for sale. It's your responsibility to buy it. Remember, keep *The Millionaire Guide* in your possession until you create financial freedom. When you do, I would like to be the first person you get in touch with.

Your friend,
DeWayne Wayne

Your next step is to join me at Culture University. Do that now.

CULTURE UNIVERSITY

(ROAD TO WEALTH COURSE)

- **The Financial Freedom Formula**
- **4 Easy steps to Create Financial Freedom**
- **Intro to Real Estate Investing**
- **How to Start Investing**
- **How to Find a Great Deal**
- **3 Ways to Analyze Real Estate**
- **How to Create Financial Freedom Investing**

Sign up today at
JOINCULTUREU.COM

Made in the USA
Monee, IL
04 November 2026

67387302R00026